CW00829295

# Whispers In Verse

# Whispers In Verse

*Cynthia A. Morgan*

Copyright (C) 2021 Cynthia A. Morgan
Layout design and Copyright (C) 2021 by Next Chapter
Published 2021 by Next Chapter
Cover art by Cover Mint
Back cover texture by David M. Schrader, used under license from Shutterstock.com
Large Print Edition
All rights reserved. No part of this book may be reproduced or transmitted in any form or by any means, electronic or mechanical, including photocopying, recording, or by any information storage and retrieval system, without the author's permission.

*For My Muse*

*Who Fills my Heart with Love*

*My Soul with Music*

*And*

*All my Passion with Words*

# Prologue

In this world of rapidity, haste, and urgency, where instant has become the norm and the norm has become tedious, the importance of Quietness and Solitude has seemingly been forgotten. We fill our daily schedules to the point where there remains little, if any, time to simply sit quietly, close our eyes, and unwind. We participate in every imaginable activity; we flutter from community event to social outing; we hurry to work, hurry to the gym, rush home, race through a meal in order to dash back out the door again until we fall into bed in the attempt to cram in a few hours of sleep before we start it all over again.

Life around us is bustling and bursting, blaring with boisterous babbling and blatantly brazen brashness that bewilders and befuddles. From the minute we bounce out of bed, we fill our eyes and ears with sound and images; we hurry our hands with smart technology; we drink copious quantities of caffeinated energy drinks so we can rush to and fro, rarely taking a moment to smell the roses or sit among the lilies. Yet Peace Pervades Peacefully. Tranquility Settles Tenderly. Serenity Rests Calmly. And the only way to attain these Treasures is to do the same.

Turn off the tunes and open the window so you may listen to the birds singing. Stop from rushing and Sigh in the warmth of the
    afternoon breeze. Forego meeting the crowd at the pub and Walk quietly along a burbling stream to listen to its purifying laughter. Turn off the lights and Gaze at the stars to wonder with awe. Put down the i-device and pick up a daisy to pluck its petals pensively or Run your hands through the feathering fronds of a whispering willow to feel tranquility seeping into your soul. Sit quietly in contemplation of the singular Majesty and Mystery of your own beating heart and Take stock of each Precious breath.

In that Quietude, where technology pauses and the human condition returns, the simple, understated gesture of folding your hands, closing your eyes, and bowing your head can have a far greater and more lasting effect upon your day and your life than any latest tune, text message, tweet, post, or energy drink. In that Silence, where all the rushing stops and a measure of Harmony returns, Peace will Pervade. Tranquility will Settle, and Serenity will Calm; teaching the mind that Opens to their gentle Presence that all the Wealth and Power in the world cannot replace the Blessing of a single moment spent Touching the Spirit.

# Contents

# Impenetrable

Measure of unchanneled Mind,
Vision of Luminous Daytide, Singing,
Wisdom of unguarded Temples,
Mystery fortified and Contemplation Bringing;
As the Hours of Night descend,
As the Glass through which we Stare, Fades,
Lustrous as the Noonday Sun,
Billows in Waves of Impenetrable Shade.
Visitor from the Limitless Beyond,
Incomparable, Beyond our ken,
Stately entrance upon the Eastern Sky,
Breath substantial, though never again.
Silence stirring in Temporal Rhyme,
Splendor dimming the stars that Shine!

# Touching The Divine

Feel the Lingering Breath of Day, Caress my
skin with Smiling,
Under the Soothing Reassurance of the Golden
Setting Sun,
Close my eyes,
Breath is Still and Calm, Sweet Repose Long
Sought,
Birdsong fills the Deepening Twilight, Echoes of
the Dawn of Time,
Darkness meets my Questing gaze in
Emptiness,

Alone,

Draw a deeper breath,
Sweet Tranquility Reaches out,
Brushes her hand across my hurried thoughts
and distracted musings,
Resting upon my Upturned cheek
As the Softest Touch of evening Unites with
rhythmic breathing,

Deep

Silent

Still

Into the Depths of Quiet Being,
Transposing the chaos of everyday into
Harmonious Liturgy,
Heartbeat sounding in my hearing,
Reminder of Precious Life,
Deeper

Quieter

Lingering Longer,

As the Gentle Touch of Your Thoughts finds me,
And Instantly I Smile,

Home

Blessed

Transformed

Time slips through the glass as Union breaks
the bonds,

Unfetters the shackles of worry and suppressed
fear,
Kisses my Spirit with Peace and Sublime
Serenity,

Inward

Placid

Abiding

Hovering Wings of Majesty,
Love Falling like misty rain, Surrounding,
Enwrapping, Invigorating,
Catalyst of Untold Alteration, Merging, Joining,
Tears of Quintessential Joy Softly Singing,

Breath

Upward

Return

Refreshed, Renewed in the Lavender Light,
Birdsong fading, Cicadas Droning, Darkness
Falling,
Eternity Calling,

Deepest, Cleansing, Stirring Sigh,
Turning my Face Toward the Starlit Sky
In the Presence of all that Truly Shines,
In Moments, Alone,
Touching the Divine.

# Unrivaled Promise

O Sweet Delirium of Time Capturing my Heart,

Spiral Faster!

Spin more Exquisitely!

Dance Upon the Night More Quickly!

Pour Forth your Mystery and Magic into this
Shallow Place,

Brightening,

Enlightening,

Whispering of Time long Past and Time yet to
Come,

Drawing The One Ever Nearer,

While I, with anticipation stealing Breath,

Wait,

Enraptured by Your Unrivaled Promise.

# Gentle Embrace

The Breath of Life Eternally Surrounds,

Tenderly Reaching,

Offering,

Holding us Ever Close.

Breathe Sweet in its Gentle Embrace,

And Live Kindly with Thankfulness.

# Simplest Balm

Morning Sings her Sweetest Song,

Enticing Daylight to Open her Eyes,

Lilting Expression through Whispers of Light,

Dramatic Flair upon Breathless Sighs.

Intoxicate my Senses, Sweet,

Infatuate my Heart and Mind,

Precious Gift of Life and Breath,

How Shall I repay this Blessing in Kind?

Choice is Driven upon the Breeze,

Bluster blowing or Zephyr Calm,

Blessing of Daytide, Spread your Joy,

Harmony in Chorus of Simplest Balm.

# Escape

Sweet Rush of Breath
Escapes,
Shivers Awaken
Longing in the Soul.
Stillness,
Silence,
Sweet Caress of the Salty Breeze,
Waiting,
Pausing,
Lingering,
Wondering,
Until another Breath,
Unhurried,
Escapes.

# Inescapable Time

This Shape of Time,
Like a Wave Does Roll,
Ever Turning the Pages,
Ever Exacting its Toll.
Pressing Us Forward,
Pushing Us Down,
Without Weight, Without Form,
Ever Spinning round.
Fleeting and Brief,
Yet Infinitely Long,
Thundering From Darkness,
Sweet as Angelic Song.
Tracing Our Days,
From First to Last Breath,
Present Before Life,
Lingering After Death,
Surrounding, Penetrating,
Inescapable Time,
Relentless Jailor,
Gentle, Loving Rhyme.

# Breathless

As the Breathless Sky, in Softness, Awaits
The Loving Kiss of the Morning Sun,
Whispers Hover in the Shadowy Mists,
Singing in Harmony with the Renewal Begun.

As the Breathless Morning, lingering, Sighs
In Quiet, Delicate Shades and Hues,
My Waking Soul Draws a Perfect Breath,
Remember Love in the Beauty of Truth.

Breathlessness beats in Serene Accord
With the Pounding Rhythm of my Soaring
Heart,
To Stand on the Mountain, in Veneration,
And Breathe in Love before the Day Starts.

# Breathe

Breathe
Slow
Gently
Know
Love
Peace
Joy
Flow
Only
Breathe
Slow
Deep

Ever
Linger
Serenity
Keep
Only
Breathe
Sweet
Free
Quietly
See
Touching
Thee.

# Ancient Story

Delicate Calm of Morning Bluster,

Revive my Heart like a rousing Muster,

Clasp my Spirit in your Gentle Embrace,

Doubts Dissolve without a Trace,

In the Shimmering Majesty of your Temperate
Glory,

Ever New, Ever Singular, Though Antediluvian
Story.

# The Mist Speaks

The Mist Speaks

Louder than Thunder

Softer than a Whisper

Caressing the skin

Running it's fingers through the hair,

Sighing in the Silence

As it Reaches Inward

Stretches Outward

Enveloping All in Bliss

Serenity

Calamity

Quiet

And Absolute Stillness.

# This Calm Quiet Place

This Calm Quiet Place, Whispering Softly;

This Peaceful Tide of Shadowy Night, Singing
Serenely;

This Tranquil Hour in Luminous Candlelight,

Speaks to my Heart in Sighs,

Telling in pale and muted tones,

All the Mysteries of the Finest Heavens,

Wrapped in Wonder and Beguiling Splendor,

While I,

Mute and Awe-struck by the Harmonious
Symphony,

Raise my veiled gaze to the Bejeweled Sky,

And Touch the Heart of God.

# Superfluous Expanse

Soft in the Silence Stretching to Heaven,

Birthed in Golden Sunlight,

Streaming Silver Incandescence,

Paradise Glimmering in the Celestial Hush,

Enigmatic Calm,

Shadow and Illusion of Temporal phase,

Superfluous Expanse of Endless Bliss,

Heaven Reaching down through Liquescent
Time,

Figment of Imagination,

Wandering in Rhyme.

# Silence Reigns

Silence is a Juncture,

A Stepping Stone to another Plane,

Where Thoughts Transcend like Liquescent
Gold,

Puddles of Musings Filling, Pouring, Spilling,

In Balmy climes and in Frozen cold,

Where Tempestuous frenzy waits in vain

To crush the Calm, To wrack and puncture,

Yet Silence Reigns where Peace Abounds,

In Tranquil, Soft, Harmonious Sounds.

# Tranquility

Tranquility Touches the Soul

And Blesses the Heart

That Opens to its Quiet Refrain

And,

In Peaceful Unison,

Sweetly Sings Along.

# Quiet Moment

Quiet Moment Closing Eyes

Breathing Sweetly

Centered Sighs

Thoughts Swirling Restive Thinking

Calming Mantra

Tranquility Linking

Peaceful Spirit Guiding Voice

Patience Increase

Purposeful Choice

Quiet Moment Closing Eyes

Breathing Sweetly

Centered Sighs

# The Whisper of the Breeze

The Whispers of the Breeze

Speaks Silence to my Heart,

In Shades of Indigo Brilliance

And Bright Luminous Mists of Tranquil Blue,

Speaking of Your Mystery,

Uttering Paradoxes, Timeless and True.

Unfettered upon this Whisper of Air,

Unchained from Grief, from Doubt, from
Despair,

Into the Realms of Pearlescent Dreams,

Glittering Incomprehensibility Streams.

# Silence - Acrostic Poem

S – Stillness, crisp and Light upon the breeze,

I – Incandescent Glitter through the leafless trees,

L – Lingering Luster of Summer's Balm,

E – Echoes of laughter in the Glistening Calm,

N – November Russets Transcending the Rush,

C – Chills Enticing through the Whispering Hush,

E – Evanescence of warmth in the December Freeze.

# The Serenity of Night

Gentle Whisper
In the Serenity of Night,
While the Stillness Softly
Makes Everything Right.
Quiet the Racing of these
Uncertain Musings,
Dancing like fireflies,
All Confusing.
Whisper through the Hush
In the Twilight Breeze,
A Lyrical Symphony
Of Softly Swaying Trees,
Under the Tenderly
Turning Skies,

Speak to my Spirit,
Eternally Wise.
Teach This Heart
To be Patient and Kind,
Help me to See
As I Walk along Blind.
Open my Ears
To the Song of the Night,
Emblazon this Life
And Make it a Light
To Shine in the Calm
Sweet Serenity of Night,
Whisper, Beloved
And Make Everything Right.

# In Stillness

In Stillness Let your Mind Unravel

From all the weary toil of Life,

Breathing Peace in Quiet Calm,

Releasing Worry, Doubt and Strife.

In Stillness Let your Heart Uplift

All its Anxious Cares and Fears,

Singing in Soft and Hushed Refrain,

Releasing Burdens in Joyful Tears.

In Stillness Let your Spirit Thrive,

Encompassing All you Say and Do,

Resting in Sweet Serenity,

Filled by Love that is Endless and True.

# Pools of the Mind

Breaths Sighing Softly, Heartbeat Lilting;

Window to the Soul closed to darkness,

Palms Open to Caress the Heavens.


These spiraling Contemplations Pause;

Thoughts Lingering o'er Sweet Subtleties,

Dreams take Flight in Deep Pools of the Mind.


Perception Soaring through the Unknown;

Demesne of Starlit Kissed Energy,

Transcend the Borders of Time and Place.

# Silence Staring

Silence Staring

Little caring

Your Sweet Peace

Beyond Comparing

Silence Listening

Tranquility Glistening

Change Delicately

Transitioning

Silence Waiting

While I Stand Debating

Wordless Hush

Softly Sedating

# Soliloquous Night

Beguiling Hush of Soliloquous Night

Transcending Harmony of Delicate Light

Enchanting Perpetually my Ineffectual Sight

# Serenade of Solitude

Dim the Candle, Burning Bright,

Into the Hush of Twilit Night,

Surrender to the Sweetest Sound,

Tumbling from the Silence,

Maligned and Drowned,

Whispers from Epochs of Time,

Calamity Spinning in Dexterous Rhyme,

In Shadows,

In Moonbeams,

Drift upon Heaven's Breast,

Serenade of Sweet Solitude

Singing me To Rest.

# Breath of Tranquility

Breath of Tranquility, Rest over me,
When I am tossed and abandoned
On the Incongruous Sea,
Imperiled, Alone, Beyond Intrepidity,
Breath of Tranquility, Sing over me,
When I am afraid, In Darkness ensnared,
Doubtful of any who ever cared,
Lingering Shadow of Superfluity,
Breath of Tranquility, Sigh over me.
Sing Sweet,
Sing Soft,
In the Heavens Aloft,
Breath of Tranquility,
Breathe Deep in Me.

# Aligned

Stir the Silence

Sweet the Hush

Cerulean Magic

Transcending the Rush

Subtle Parlance

Of Mystery Undefined

Musical Whisper

With Heaven Aligned

# Billows of Time

Billows of Time,

Whirling in Rhyme,

Concentric Circles of Wandering Light,

Immutable Treasure,

Boundless Measure

Expanding my Wearisome, Limited Sight.

# Quiet

Quiet,
Gentle Wealth of Heaven,

Touching
The Chaos of my Spirit,

Soothe,
Like Balm of Liquid Love,

Whisper
So my Unrest will Hear it.

Quiet,
Incorporeal Temperance,

Sustain
The Repose of my Heart,

Settle
Softly like the Hush of Snow,

Sleep
In Serenity that does not Depart.

Quiet,
Purest Placid Glow,

Illuminate
The fractured way,

Silently
Speak in subdued tones,

Sigh,
With Peace to Fill my Day.

# The Hush

It is the Still, Soft Hush that Speaks the Loudest.

It is the Gentle, Quiet Peace that Reaches the Deepest.

It is the Tender, Soothing Serenity that Comforts the Greatest.

# Hues

Shifting Hues Like Shadow Play

Across the Luminous Breaking Day,

Echoes of a Glimmering Time

When Harmony walked

Hand in Hand with Rhyme.

Brilliance Falls on the Misty Morn,

Prismatic Colours to Adorn

The Shifting Hues of Memory

Calling out Across Fields

Of Verdant Serenity.

Dipped in Kaleidoscopic Shade,

Hills of Reverence Gloriously Displayed.

# Quiet Hour

Rest

Trust

Sigh

Drift

Cleanse

Eternal

Healing

The Rift

Pulse

Rush

Solitude

Quiet Hour

Harmony

Transcend

Uniting

Eternal Power

Rest

Trust

Breathe

Sigh

Dream

BE

Unleash

Fly

# Silence Bending

Hearken, then, to the Unspoken Call

Whispering from Shadow and Shade,

Folds of Silence Bending from russet Fall,

Twilight Glimmering Crimson, from which it's made.

While Worries Sleep
And Memories Keep,

Magic Weaves Wonder 'midst the Sparkling Glade.

# Silence in its Golden Hour

Silence is

In All its Golden Hour

Reverence cast Adrift upon the

Ever Shifting Tide of Night;

That in its Reverie

All that once was Said,

Though Played in mischief

Might come to Light.

# Tranquility Rests

Tranquility Rests, Gently Sighing,

Waiting for the Heart to cease its crying,

Wailing always Woe is Me

To Bless and Restore like the Endless Sea,

In the Palest Hour,

In the Harrowing Storm,

Tranquility Rests

Never to Conform

But Breathing Softly in the chaotic Fray,

Tranquility Rests,

Quiet Peace to Convey.

# Time Unfolding

Beauty Speaking

Sweet Quietude

Memory Breathing

Peaceful Solicitude

Ages Bending

Earthly Hues

Time Unfolding

Subtly Infuse

# Soft in the Silence

Soft in the Silence,
Mute Wonder Behold,
Whispering Mysteries,
Languid,
Untold,
Creation Stooping
To Grasp the Sound,
As Softness Speaks Quietly,
All Around.
Touching the Heart,
Calming Fear,
Reminding,
Reassuring,
Peace is Near.

# Ocean's Sigh

Night stands Silent,

The Air is Still,

The Waves are Subtle,

Insubstantial.

Peace Transcends

The Mortal Rush,

Stars wink softly

Setting Sun's Pink Blush.

The Ocean Breathes,

Spiraling Terns Cry,

Sand And Salt,

Breathless Sigh.

# Lush Emeraldine

Beyond the Chasm of Earthly Tones,
Of browns and russets and sables,
A Broad, Viridian Enchantment Waits,
Filled with Magic and Mysteries and Fables.
Sweet Breath of Lusciously Verdant Hues,
Delicate Scent of Fragrant Green,
Pause, Close your eyes, Inhale Deep and Slow,
Beguile your senses with the Voluptuous Scene.
Walk Quietly among the Jade Symphony,
Listen, Enchanted, to Echoing Birdsong,
Lie back in the Plush Velvet Tapestry,
Dream Luxurious Dreams, Fair and Long.
Sigh in the Lush Emeraldine Embrace,
Forgetting Time, Abandoning Place.

# Subtle

Colours of Silk,

Soft Hues' Shifting Sand,

Silence Lifting

Like the Most Gentle Hand.

Moonlight Singing

Of Distant Dreams;

Lavender Mantle,

Melancholy Themes.

Mist of Whispers,

Reflection of Light,

Subtle, Silvery,

Lullaby Night.

# The Whispers

Listen to the Softest sound,

The Hum of History Speaking loud,

In the dusky, earthen shroud,

Or in the Vision of Liberating Green.


Past the intricate technology,

Beyond the Fine, Posh Luxury,

Into the Picturesque Vistas I See,

Glimmering in an Archaic Sheen.


Speaking in Tones Gently Untold,

While the future hurries to unfold,

I Stand on the hillside, Silent and Bold,

Listening to the Whispering Scene.

# Spectacle of Heaven

Infinite Splendor

In Majestic Miniature,

Breathless Wonder

Of Love, Ever Sure,

Delicate Harmony

In Fleeting Serenity,

Spectacle of Heaven

Abides in You and Me.

# Whispering Silence

Silence

.

Whispering

.

Brilliance

.

Reflecting

.

Tranquility

.

Whispering

.

Silence

# Tender Blush

Tender Blush
Of Shy Sweet Colour,
Kiss my Memory
With your Delicate Flourish,
Linger in the Quietness of my Dreams
With Sweetness of Honeyed Scent
And Tapestries of Hues,
Ever Shifting in Dulcet Romance
To Enchant my Days with
Subtle Tantalization
That turns my senses from their melancholy
chaos
To Drops of Fragrant Harmony Singing in
Reflection of Your Absolute Beauty.

# Where Soliloquy Sings

There is a place I Hide my Heart

Where Silence Glimmers and Serenity Reigns,

A Place that Sparkles with Luminescent Light,

Where Negativity Sits Mute and ne'er
Complains.

Echoes of Giggles Fill these Halls

And Dancing Cherubs on Fluttering Wings,

Where Poets Chant their Rhymes and Reasons

With Fluted Tones While Soliloquy Sings.

Mermaids Splash and Rainbows Drip

Their Colours Down Like Candied Rain,

Soft in the Shadows Happiness Waits,

Transporting me from the Weary Mundane.

# Palest Hour

Palest Hour

Shade of Night

Tumultuous Colour

Blissful Delight

Whisper of Tranquility

Blazing Passion in Serenity

Singing Morn

Unsullied Twilight

Liquescent Splendour

Shimmering Bright

Secret of Equanimity

Breathless Abandon in Anonymity

# Celestial Garden

Blooming in Flowers

of Bright Serenity,

Fire in the Welcoming Arc

Expanding Over Me.

Overwhelming Beauty

Bringing Tears to the Seeking Eye,

Celestial Garden Flourishing

Bright Poppies in the Sky.

# Spirit of the Whispering Night

Spirit of the Whispering Night

Silence

Tranquility

Far Distant Light

Heavens Bending to Caress the Soul

Inescapable

Perception

Harmonious Cosmic Shoal

# Drape

Drape
Of Silence
In the Rush
Whispering
Drape
Of Mesmerizing Hush
Drape
Of softness
Delicate of Hue
Tantalizing
Enchanting
Breathless view
Drape
Of All
I Long to See
Drape
My Mind
Until I am Free!

# Silence Reaches

Silence Reaches,
Stretching through Time,
Through Mysteries,
Through Shadows,
Signifying Rhyme;
Silence Whispers,
Harmonizing in the Calm,
Reminding,
And Binding,
With Tranquility's Balm;
Silence Glimmers,
Singing Softly of Yore;
Entrancing,
Romancing,
As Silence Reaches Evermore.

# Silence Purity Beauty

Silence
Dripping from Heaven
Purity
Settling amid the Hush
Beauty
Scattering the Gloom
Tranquility
Softly Beguiling
Silence
Dance Upon the Breeze
Purity
Cascading from Grayness
Beauty
Whispering Chills
Tranquility
Echoing Lullaby in
Silence

# Companion

Shades of Thought, Quietly Transcending,
Lilting Echoes of Light, Bending,
Song of Ancient Memory, Sing,
Paradox unto Thy Companion, Bring;
Whispers of the Daytide, Softly Borrow,
Forgotten until the Rise of Tomorrow,
While All the world beneath Thy Haze,
Nod their heads in a Blissful Daze.
True Companion, Ever Tending,
Quietly,
Sweetly,
Silently Bending,
Beguile and Tempt; With Starlight Infuse,
Employ Thy Gaze to Lovingly Confuse.

# I Sing

I Sing
When there is Silence
In the Breath of the Shimmering Night.
I Sing
Where there is Calmness
In the Glimmer of Expansive Starlight.

I Sing
When there is Birdsong
Joyous in its Sweet Calamity.
I Sing
Where there is Spilling Rain
In Gentle Whispers of Tranquility.

I Sing
After the Storm has Broken
In the Crescendo of thunderous Sound.
I Sing
As the Winds twist and bluster
Spinning like a maelstrom round.

I Sing
At the foot of the mountain
Gazing up to the Spiraling Heights
I Sing
When I hear Your Echo,
A Memory of Ancient Delights.

# Beneath and Beyond

As the Winds Moan and Sigh

And the Gales of this world

Rock this tiny skiff and billow its Sails,

The Nighttide Sings Sweetly

Beneath Effervescent Stars

That Glister through Untold Distances;

Beyond this Silhouette of Silence,

Past the Echoes of Forgotten Memory,

Light Pours through the Expanse,

Seeking,

Touching,

Warming,

All.

# Soft Silence

Soft Silence

Singing,

Mimicking the Past,

Listening through Heartbeats,

Where Memory is Cast

Adrift upon the Ocean,

Playing Melody

Lilting,

Clear,

Silence Softly Intoning

Wisdom for the Soul to Hear.

# Garden of Stars

Garden of Stars

Burning in my Dreams,

Luminous Daffodils in Silence Blooming,

Ribbons of Eternity, Streaming in Midnight,

Paint your Colours into my Heart

As Flowers Scent the Dappled darkness,

Brightening this Path upon which I mutely
tread

Like a Verdant Avenue of Hope.

# Beguiling Night

Drift upon the tide of Night,

Indigo Whispers Upon Ebon Dreams,

Reality Lapsing into Cosmic Light,

Twilight Glistening through Heavenly Seams,

Sleep and Dream while Tranquility Bends,

Beguiling Night where Mystery Ascends.

# Shimmering Show

She Pours out her Love for All to See,
Blushing Beneath the Silvered Skies,
Dancing in Ethereal, Glistening Streaks,
Upon the Luminous Hush of Night.

Spilling Her Incandescent Caress,
Like a Bride Bedecked in Shimmering Show,
Ever Faithful in her Course, Unless,
Dark Masquerade Transforms her Radiant
Glow.

Then, Behold, her Tender Touch
In Crimson Hue, turns Ruddy and Bold,
Intoxicating, like drinking Wine too much,
Yet Fleeting, like Youth before growing old.

Yet when Her Shimmering Light Spreads Wide
Upon the Breathless, Waiting Night,
'Tis Loveliness Unfettered which Presides,
While we Stare in Wonder at the Enthralling
Sight.

# The River of Time

Silence comes in Shadows and Rocky Pools

Where Light Reflects the Glimmering facets

Of Hope and Faith,

Courage Shimmering on the surface of the
waters,

Even beneath the canopy of Overhanging fear;

Ever Shifting,

Ever Rushing onward

In the 'plash of the River of Time.

# Silence Speaks

Silence Speaks

Long and Slow

Deep and Low

Whispering

Things I Do not Know

Silence Speaks

In Willows, Waving

Like Caresses Upon the Shore

Deliberate

Intractable

Ever Wanting More.

# Silence Stirring

Silence Stirring like Channels of rain,

Pattering upon the sill of my Soul,

Washing away rivers of pain,

Transforming deep oceans to Glittering shoal.

Echoes Pouring like Ribbons of Light,

Dancing upon the Wings of my Heart,

Lifting up the wrong with the Right,

Enlightenment to Gently Impart.

Shadows casting Rainbows of Sound

Into my ever Watchful gaze,

Perplexity spinning my Thoughts Around,

From Beginning to End, Guiding my Days.

# Shades of Midnight

Shades of Midnight Stir,

Collapsing in on Darker Shadows,

Spiraling like Wisps of smoke

Around the fragmentary Echoes of

My Memories;

Chasing Harlequin Desire

Down Diamond-studded corridors,

Thirsting for Elaborate,

Yet Hungry for Quintessence.

# Ethereal Galleon

Starlight Sails like an
Ethereal Galleon,
Riding the Waves on the
Ebon Night,
Chasing my Dreams
Through the Glistening Spangle,
Cresting the Waves of
Lavender Twilight.
Rocking in my Imagination,
Gentle Apparition Sailing,
Reciting Sonnets To the
Open Heavens,
My Questing Spirit
Ever Regaling.
Silhouette of Solicitude,
Paint Your way Across the Sky,
While the Serenading Moon
Weaves and Smiles,
With A Seraphic
Tranquil Sigh.

# Magnificence

Magnificence Dances upon the Daytide,

Splendour in Brilliant, Sparkling Array.

Magnificence Graces each Breathless Sigh,

Entreating Trust to cast fears away.

Magnificence Bends in Gentle fashion,

Mighty Spirit of Tranquility.

Magnificence Blazes with Beauteous Passion,

Entrusting Magnificence to me.

# Enigmatic Dreams

Splendor of Enigmatic Dreams,

Conjuring Magic beyond Realistic Themes,

Dancing Light of Heaven, Bending,

Tranquility to my Spirit, Tending,

Sorcery Spilling from the Singing Sky,

Ethereal,

Blissful,

Endless Sigh.

# Whispers of Transpiring Night

Whispers of Transpiring Night,

Singing Luminance of Shimmering Light,

Guardian of Eternal Hours,

Walking, Whispering, Among the Flowers

Of All we Long to Ever Be,

Of All we Strive for and Hope to See,

Whispers Chanting in the Lavender Night,

Singing, Immortal, Transcending Delight.

# Nighttide - Diamante

Nighttide

Enduring Synchronicity

Whispering, Engendering, Transcending

Velveteen Magic, Mystery Afar

Sparkling, Scintillating, Life-Giving,

Breathtaking Splendor

Stars

# Moonlight

Moonlight is Dancing
At the edge of my Sight.
Drifting like shadows Cast into the fray;
Tempting me to close my eyes,
Weaving Magic Unparalleled by day.

Starlight is Drifting
Through my Waking Fancy.
Casting their Light Upon the morn;
Entreating me to Gaze up wonderingly
To the Place where Souls are Born.

Twilight is Transcending,
Like Whispers to my Inner Peace.
Chanting like primal Melody, Singing;
Eluding to Murmurs yet to come,
And All the shivers they are Bringing.

# Ignite

Starlight Sparkling

Darkened Night

Creation of Heaven Shimmering Bright

Magic Shimmering

Ethereal Light

Inspiration of Whispering Twilight

Harmony Blending

Glistening Sight

Unification Enchantingly Ignite

# Cosmos – Cinquain

Tranquil

Sweet Starlit Night

Whispers from the Heavens

Fill the Heart and Soul with Wonder

Cosmos

# Tower of Night

Tower of Night,

Dark river of Dreams,

Thundering Melody of Timeless Symphony.

Echo of Memory,

Enticing Fragile Thought,

Intoxicating Beauty, with Mortal Danger
Fraught.

Spectacle of Heaven,

Gleaming Majesty,

Claim my Inspiration with Deliberate Mystery!

# Midnight

The Candle is dimming as Midnight Bears her
head,
Letting her Cascading Tresses tumble forth
upon the Night,
Sighing Deeply, she Raises her hands slowly
over her head,
Releasing from her Gentle Grasp the Diamonds
of Light she Holds,
Scattering Temptation that Sparkles and
Glitters in the Hush.

In the Shifting Shades the Dim Hours Sing from
Vastness,
She Sways and Turns in subtle, slow
Suspirations,
Smiling in the Whispering blackness,
Wrapping her arms around her Lover,
Hesitant to waken him with the Breath of Morn
As she watches him Dream.

# Mesmerize

Silhouette of shifting gold,

Echoes of Memories both new and Old,

Trailing Lantern through the Quizzical Night,

Bold, Defiant, Sweet Gentle Light,

Cascading ribbon of Ethereal Rhyme,

Whispering of epochs of Mystical Time,

Stately Sojourner, Quietly Guiding,

From Fierce Apollo Demurely Hiding,

Enraptured by Thee, I Tend the Night Hours,

Like a Garden of Blissful, Delicate Flowers,

Emblazoned into the Heart of me,

Mesmerizing Enchantress,

Setting me Free.

# Weep Not For Me

Weep Not for me,
When Darkness Falls I Shall be free,
Free to Dance in the Painted Night,
Free to Caress the Sky with Light,
Touching Dreams with my Softest Smile,
Intoxicating Gazes with my Enchanting Guile,
Weep Not for this Long Hour of Sleep,
Waiting, Silent, with the Secrets I Keep,
As the Heaven's are Endlessly Turning
And the Seas I ride are Tempestuously churning,
Weep Not for Me,
For When Darkness Falls I Shall be Free.

# Imparting Harmony

With Glints of Moonlight upon the Wall,
A Cradle of Elegant Starlight, Glistens,
Watchful Heartbeats as they Fall,
Where Angels Pause as Faiths Listens.

Tender in the Midnight Calm
Of Jocund Candleglow a-shimmer,
Softly, now, in Whispered Balm,
While doubt and fear grow dimmer.

The Pulsing of Celestial Wonder,
Stealing from Infinity so Far,
Beckons my Gaze like Joyous Thunder,
Or the Fleetly Falling Brittle Star.

Yet in Comparison of Day to Night,
Untold the Secrets Tending,
Luster fades as Day Breaks so Bright,
And Passion's Ministrations, Bending.

Arch Your Gilded Wings, Oh Heaven,
Spread Your Wisdom like the Deepest Sea,
Food of Immortality, Sweetly Leaven,
Quietly Imparting Harmony.

# Veil of Morning

Veil of Morning Light,

Shimmering Essence, Gentle and Bright,

Caress my waking Mind with Sighs,

As the Whispering shade of Nighttide flies,

Lingering Traces of Remembered Dreams

Biding their Time as Delicate Hope Gleam

# Stillness

Stillness In Blue,

Indigo for me, Lavender for You,

Poised on the Precipice Of Placidly Quiet Calm,

Dancing Rosy Prisms

Whispering Balm.

# By The Hours

By Hour of Sweetest Night,
When Daytide, Blushing, turns her Fair Cheek
away,
And All the Heavens, do, in Spectral Show,
Dance to the eye and Court each Heart with
Smiles;
My Lingering Breath,
Which in heaves and sighs Permits this Life
Continuance,
Calls my Waiting and Long Yearning Riotous
Calamity
And Curses All the Happy Hours that chortle
and mock her Breathless Vigil.

By Morning's Jocund Light,
When Midnight, Sleeping, Hides her Veiled
Gaze,
And All the Larks in Beauteous Gardens and
Blithe canopies of Viridian,
Sing to the Blessed Heavens with Lusty Peals
and Vigor;
My Bleary Gaze,
Which Watches through Sweet Floods of tears
as Life Persists,
Belies the Droll humour of my Lips
That in Laughing and Light Revelry makes such
Misery
As this Heart would, else, endlessly cry, False.

Yet, By the Breath of Twilight,
When Labours Cease and Silence,
For One Fleeting Measure,
Like the Soothing Caress of a Lover's Hand
That in his Lightest Touch does Ease the
Sorrows of the Day and Burdens of the Mind,
A Balm as Sweet as Dulcet Wine to the Lip and
As Fine as the Harmonious Melodies of the
Lute,
Fills Each Lingering Breath with Sighs,
Dries the Water from these Searching eyes,
When in that Shifting Light, 'neath the
Lavender Whispers of Eventide,
I See Your Most Beguiling Smile.

# Simplest Balm

Morning Sings her Sweetest Song,

Enticing Daylight to Open her Eyes,

Lilting Expression through Whispers of Light,

Dramatic Flair upon Breathless Sighs.

Intoxicate my Senses, Sweet,

Infatuate my Heart and Mind,

Precious Gift of Life and Breath,

How Shall I repay this Blessing in Kind?

Choice is Driven upon the Breeze,

Bluster blowing or Zephyr Calm,

Blessing of Daytide, Spread your Joy,

Harmony in Chorus of Simplest Balm.

# Whispering Pillow of Softest Air

Whispering Pillow of Softest Air,
Embracing the Garden with Delicate Flair,
Reaching Tenderly to Take my Hand,
Enshrouding the Curves and Temptations
Of Land,
Speaking Quietly to my Attentive ear,
Whispering Mysteries I am
Too Deaf to Hear,
Rose Hued Shade of Morning's Love,
Tempting Warmth Descend from High Above,
Stand Gracious in Your Shimmering Hour
Like Calliope's Lyre, a Lyrical Flower,
Blushing and Delicate in Pristine Youth,
Revealing Sparkling, Enigmatic Truth.
Oh! Allow my Gaze to Linger There
Upon You Sweet Mists, To Sigh and Stare!

# Path

Path
Of Canyons,
Shadows
Of Shale,
Thunderstorm
Singing,
Raining Bright Hail,
Rock
Of Chasms,
Echo
Of Deep Calm,
Calamitous

Whisper,
Shouting Sweet Balm,
Moment
Of Tomorrow,
Yesterdays Swale,
Timeless Promise
Unbreakably Frail.
Path
of Deep Ocean,
Trail
Of Sweet Tears,
Impossible Harmony
Cascade of Years.

# Soft Silence

Soft Silence Singing,

Mimicking the Past,

Listening through Heartbeats where Memory is
Cast

Adrift upon the Ocean,

Lilting,

Clear,

Silence Softly Intoning

Wisdom for the Soul to Hear.

# Remembrance

Reaching Across the distant shores,

Bending to inaccessible Stars,

Hours Shifting,

Sands Sifting,

Through Immutable Scars;

Memory Lying Fallow,

Shards of Bleak Time,

Harbinger of discord,

Perspective of Rhyme,

Singing sweetly in the Intrinsic Hush,

Ever Listening,

Ever Waiting,

Desolate And Lush!

# Memory and Time

Sweet and Beautiful

Spellbinding Gaze

Lost in the Mirror of Your Halcyon daze

Beguilingly Piquant

Sensuously Fair

Inexpressibly Charming with Youthful Flair

Enchanting Dilemma

Memory and Rhyme

Unbroken Alliance severing Time.

# Tapestry of Twilight

Tapestry of Twilight,

Delicately Infuse,

Trace your Fingers through my Thoughts

To Suffuse

Intrinsic Memory of

Whispers, Unspoken,

Vortex Speaking of Boundaries Unbroken,

Calling my Heart,

Touching my Dreams,

Beyond Understanding of what it Means,

Tapestry of Twilight,

Spiraling, Offer,

Passage Beyond

Where Mortals Bow and Proffer.

# Memory Dances

Memory Dances Upon Silken Wings,

Even in the Shadow of Darkness and Despair,

Beguiling,

Bewitching As it Sings,

Renewing,

Transforming Beyond Compare.

# The Wondering Bystander

Beyond Morning

Into Memory so Sweet,

Time Eclipsed by Time Alone,

Standing mute Testament to All Those She has
Touched,

Empty vessels, broken pieces,

Lingering Evidence of Her Passage,

Bending Perception with the slanting Light,

In which She Dances,

Merging Past and Present to Kiss the forehead
of

The Wondering Bystander.

# Memory Lingers

Memory,

Like the Tidal Sea,

Lingers Breathlessly in me;

Shifting,

Like Waves upon the Shore,

Whispering Patiently, More and More.

Memory,

Like the Azurine Deep,

Reminds me of the Secrets I Keep;

Dancing,

Like the Endless Ocean,

Waxing and Waning in Perpetual Motion.

# Beyond

Beyond

The Shadows that Flicker and Dance;

Beyond

The Doubt of never taking the Chance;

Beyond

Trepidation's Icy Stare;

Beyond

Negativity's Extravagant Flair;

Beyond

The Echoes of Uncertainty,

Abides

The Glimmer of Magical Reality,

If the Guise of Intrepidity

Beyond

Is Donned.

# Quest

Time is a Coalescence
Of All that Once was Dreamed,
Pulling at Reality and
All that Might Have Been.

Time is Unification of
All that Can Be Envisioned,
All that Might be Conjured and
Most of what should be shunned.

Each Emotion, whether Bitter or Sweet,
Turing through the Chasm,
Every Thought, Mute or Complete,
Like Shifting, Ghostly Phantasm.

Marching in Eternal Progression
Toward All that Yet May Be,
Ever Granting Bold Concession
In the Quest for Harmony.

# The Face of the Moon

In the Vast congregation of Incorporeal Time

These Dreams have shifted,

Incongruous Rhyme.

Filtering from Eternity like Shards of Glass,

While Heaven on both sides of me

Seems to Pass,

While I, Standing,

Waiting,

Neither Late, nor Too Soon,

Behold the Sweet Splendor Of the Face of the
Moon.

# Waves of Time

Waves of Time

Like Ripples in Stone,

Expose Perpetual Change

With Permanent Evidence

That Fade in the Grasp

Of Waves of Time

# Intricacies of Speculation

Space Belies no Limitless Ending,

Time Separates not from Eternity,

Chapters Spun in this Endless Frame

Cast Existence Upon a Wheel of Perpetual
Clockwork,

Delving into the Intricacies of Speculation

To Commune with Deities

And Bend our Fragile Imaginations.

# In Realms of Time

In Realms of Time

Beyond Mortal Rhyme

Where Light and consciousness Bend,

Mystery Sublime

Like Harmonious Chimes

Serenade Melodically without End.

# Timeless Parade

Layers of Night

Sky and Shade

Billowing Majesty of Timeless Parade

Golden Fire

Celestial Splendor

Mighty Artistry to Breathlessly Render

Layers of Daytide

Entreating to Borrow

Yesterday Singing of Promising Tomorrow

# Time Paints

Time Paints Each Day

With Tender Moments and Sparkling Promise,

Allowing Us to Choose to See

Beauty,

Challenge,

or Adversity.

# Kingdom of Dreams

In the Starless Heavens Waits

The Monarch of the Nightly Realm,

Riding through the Mists of Time

Upon a Ship of Ebon Sighs,

With Dreams of Stately Yesteryear

Murmuring at the Helm,

Where Solitude Breathes Quiet Repose

and Silently Implies:

Time is but a Sojourner

In the Ocean of Reality,

Opening this Kingdom of Dreams

To Calm our Fears and Set us Free.

# The Ebon Leviathan

Upon the Sleepy tide of Night,
With Indigo Shade upon my Sails;
A Thousand Diamonds cast their Light,
While the Ebon Leviathan sweetly Exhales.

The Celestial Galleon gently Sways,
Weaving Her way 'cross Sappharine Seas;
Through the Sparkling 'scape, Hyperion Plays,
While the Ebon Leviathan rhythmically
Breathes.

My Gaze entreats the Crystal Expanse,
Seeking the Sojourner brightly Ablaze.
Intoxicating Venus, he Parades his Dance,
While the Ebon Leviathan, Smitten, Obeys.

The Rigging Whispers an Ancient Tale,
Echoes Lost in the Unfathomable Deep.
I Stand Entranced, Trembling and Pale
Watching the Ebon Leviathan Sleep.

# Kiss

Long her Journey Quietly Guides her

'Cross the Vast Expanse of Time,

Ruled by her Immortal Partner,

Rocking Gently in Synchronous Rhyme,

As the Tapestry of Glittering Night

Drifts Silently Upon Unfurled Sails,

She Smiles Delicately in Grandeur,

While the Heaven's Enchantingly Unveils

All its Mystery, Beguiling and Sweet,

Parading in the Infinite Abyss,

Nightly Sojourn that E'er Romances,

Ending with Her Lingering Kiss.

# What Are You Made Of

Lift Up your eyes to the Sea of Stars,

So close Inside you and yet so Far.

Look Down upon the Humble Earth,

Remember her Arms that Gave you Birth.

Look Inside at your Spirit Unending,

See Heaven to Earth Eternally Bending.

# Dreams Be Sweet

Evening has Dispelled its Lavender,

Moonlight Pirouettes with Sparkling Light,

As I, in Weary Consecration,

Nodding, Do Quietly Bid Thee, Good Night.

Dreams Be Sweet Upon Thy Pillow,

May Starlight Kiss Thy Blushing Cheek,

Drift in Careless Slumber, Softly,

Until Breaking Dawn Thy Gaze Does Seek.

# Eternity Singing

There is a Quietude to the Embers of Night
That drifts through my Memory,
Spilling its Peaceful Melody
Into the Frenzy of my turbulent Sight.
Cascading Ribbons of Violet Haze
Reach from Heaven to, thus, Entrance me,
While Softest Mists of Starlight Glaze
The whirl of my Distracted energy.
Spinning Cosmic Ocean of Dreams
Turn my Thoughts to Peaceful Rest,
While You Sing Eternally
Of Life,
Of Renewal,
Of One Single Breath.

# Descend

Descend

Sweet Silence

Upon my Brash Calamity,

Descend

Purest Peace

With Harmonious Tranquility,

Descend

Gentle Grace

Into my thrashing notions,

Descend

Soft Stillness

Like the Scintillating Ocean.

# Epilogue

So often I write with my eyes closed, waiting. Hands poised over the keys (of my laptop), ready. Heart quiet in restful calm or pounding in passionate inspiration, and Spirit open, willing, questing, seeking, listening, as the words and images come tumbling down. Down from Heaven, down from the sweet, sparkling heavens, down from the clouds of thundering rain, down from the mountaintop, down from the breathless moon and silken skies.

There I am, an open vessel; a cracked vase that cannot hold this rushing flood, yet I can channel it, direct it into the pages of my memory. As I sit quietly, waiting; or desperately trying to keep up with the rushing torrent, my spirit sings the sweetest tune I have ever heard. And, though I cannot physically hear it, though I cannot listen to the manifestation of music like I do when I connect to my playlists, I hear the serenade as clearly as that faltering music. The melody comes down, Down from Heaven, down from the sweet, sparkling heavens, down from the clouds of glittering glow, down from the bastion towering o'er the rushing ocean's flow.

Eyes closed, waiting. Heart Quiet, listening. Spirit Willing, Questing. All for the lyrical beauty that spills like an endlessly cascading fall of sparkling water from that inestimably breathtaking Source. Typing, typing as fast as I am able, unconcerned about spelling, punctuation, context, verbiage. I sit in humble wonder as the blessed words pour Down. Down from Heaven. Down from the Sweet, Sparkling heavens. Down from the rainbow of jubilant Promise arching over all of us. Down from the crystal cerulean skies as they weep blessed words, and I am left to cry.

Cry at the beauty expressed through my hands. Weep for the Love, I hope ONE may understand. Cry in joy for the unspeakable gift that raises my life from the darkest rift into which I had fallen for many long years. A rift flooded with unshed tears. Yet now those tears flow down like rain. Down without the crushing pain and they speak in a voice so many can hear, they speak quietly, yet they speak clear. They rush and they flow like the ocean's roar, like rain falling down in a heavy pour. Down, down, Down From Heaven, Down from the Sweet Sparkling heavens, Down from the Stars that shimmer and glow, Down in a jocund, rejoicing, inexpressible flow into which I am cast, like a fisher of words. And Casting my net, I haul them in to be heard.

Dear reader,

We hope you enjoyed reading *Whispers In Verse*. Please take a moment to leave a review, even if it's a short one. Your opinion is important to us.

Discover more books by Cynthia A. Morgan at https://www.nextchapter.pub/authors/cynthia-morgan-fantasy-author

Want to know when one of our books is free or discounted? Join the newsletter at http://eepurl.com/bqqB3H

Best regards,
Cynthia A. Morgan and the Next Chapter Team

# About The Author

Cynthia A. Morgan is an award-winning author; free-lance writer, blogger, poet and up-and-coming podcaster. Currently working with GoldenNetwork.TV in a project that will make her dystopian fantasy *Mercy Series* and her young adult fantasy *Dark Fey Trilogy* available globally via ROKU, Morgan's captivating tales serve as a backdrop for powerful messages like 'show thankfulness through kindness and appreciate blessings through generosity' and 'the only way to achieve peace is by becoming peace'.

Morgan is also the creator of the popular blogs *Booknvolume* and *Word Mongery and Musings* where over 18,000 followers regularly explore Morgan's own brand of poetry, musings about life, photography, book reviews and more. Upcoming projects include a fictional drama in Regency Period England, a non-fiction exploration of the supernatural/paranormal and beliefs we share as one Human culture, and a return to the realms of Dark Fey in a mind-bending prequel.

When asked how she feels about writing, Morgan has said: "To write; to paint with words as an artist bedecks his canvas with hues and shades and layers of pigmentation; to sing a melody upon which the gaze may linger and over which the heart may muse again and again: to create visual splendor with grammar and language is the most beguiling form of intoxication in which I could ever take pleasure."

You can find Morgan through social media in the following places:

Blogs:
www.booknvolume.com
&
https://wordmongeryandmusings.com
Amazon Author Page:
Author.to/CAMorganAuthor
Official Author Website:
https://www.cynthiaamorganauthor.com/
Twitter:
https://www.twitter.com/MorganBC728
Facebook
https://www.facebook.com/booknvolume

Pinterest:
https://www.pinterest.com/creativiapub/
author-board-cynthia-a-morgan/
GoodReads:
https://www.goodreads.com/author/show/
14174277.Cynthia_A_Morgan
Publisher's Author Page:
https://www.nextchapter.pub/authors/cynthia-
morgan-fantasy-author

Whispers In Verse
ISBN: 978-4-86751-170-1 (Large Print)

Published by
Next Chapter
1-60-20 Minami-Otsuka
170-0005 Toshima-Ku, Tokyo
+818035793528
19th July 2021

Lightning Source UK Ltd.
Milton Keynes UK
UKHW021154190821
389111UK00002B/13